Christmas at Buttermilk Basin

19 Patterns for Mini-Quilts and More

Stacy West

Martingale®
Create with Confidence

Christmas at Buttermilk Basin:
19 Patterns for Mini-Quilts and More
© 2019 by Stacy West

Martingale®
19021 120th Ave. NE, Ste. 102
Bothell, WA 98011-9511 USA
ShopMartingale.com

Printed in China
24 23 22 21 20 19   8 7 6 5 4 3 2 1

Library of Congress Cataloging-in-Publication Data
is available upon request.

ISBN: 978-1-68356-003-6

MISSION STATEMENT

We empower makers who use fabric and yarn to make life more enjoyable.

CREDITS

**PUBLISHER AND
CHIEF VISIONARY OFFICER**
Jennifer Erbe Keltner

CONTENT DIRECTOR
Karen Costello Soltys

DESIGN MANAGER
Adrienne Smitke

MANAGING EDITOR
Tina Cook

PRODUCTION MANAGER
Regina Girard

TECHNICAL EDITOR
Nancy Mahoney

**COVER AND
BOOK DESIGNER**
Kathy Kotomaimoce

COPY EDITOR
Kathleen Cubley

LOCATION PHOTOGRAPHER
Adam Albright

STUDIO PHOTOGRAPHER
Brent Kane

ILLUSTRATOR
Sandy Loi

SPECIAL THANKS
*Photography for this book was taken at
Carol Hansen's Garden Barn in Indianola, Iowa.*

Contents

3 Use one strand of pearl cotton to blanket-stitch the larger pieces in place, matching the floss color to the motif. On small pieces, you might prefer to use one or two strands of floss and a whipstitch. Use three strands of green floss to blanket-stitch around the wreaths. Use tan-and-cream twisted tweed to blanket-stitch around the second, third, and fifth trees.

Appliqué placement

Embellishing the Design

Refer to "Embroidery Stitches" on page 78 as needed and use three strands of floss throughout.

- **Trees 3 and 5:** Use green floss to chain stitch the centerline and branches, green floss and a straight stitch for the needles, and red floss to make a French knot at the end of each branch.

- **Wreaths:** With rose floss, make French knots for berries. At the bottom of each wreath and using red floss, insert the needle from the front and then bring it up from the back, leaving two long tails. Tie the ends into a bow, and then trim any excess from the tails.

- **Snowman:** Use black floss to make French knots for the eyes, mouth, and buttons; orange floss and a chain stitch for the carrot nose; and brown floss and a chain stitch or stem stitch for arms.

- **Snowflakes in the sky:** Cross-stitch with cream floss.

- **Button string of lights:** Thread a needle with the black-and-white twine and knot one end, then come up from the back at the top of the left

<hr>

pole. Drape the twine as shown in the photo above, inserting the needle at the top of the pole on the right. Tie off on the back.

- **Buttons:** Referring to the photo above, sew five red ⅜" buttons over the twine to secure it, five 3 mm red buttons to the tree for bulbs, a cream ⅜" button at the top of each pole, and the ¼" cream button to the snowman's hat for a tassel.

Finishing

1 Trim the appliquéd rectangle to measure 10" × 16½", keeping the design centered. Center and pin the appliquéd rectangle on the right side of one of the red rectangles. Use three strands of black-and-tan twisted tweed floss to blanket-stitch around the perimeter of the appliquéd rectangle to secure it to the red background.

2 Pin the appliquéd piece and remaining red rectangle right sides together. Stitch the pieces together using a ¼" seam allowance, leaving a 4" opening to turn the runner. Clip the corners and turn the runner right side out. Stitch the opening closed.

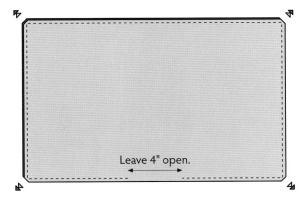

Leave 4" open.

JOY Stocking Set

A petite trio of stockings makes for charming holiday decor. They're even big enough for tucking in some small goodies, such as chocolates, note cards, fat quarters, or other trinkets and treasures.

> **Finished size: 5⅜" × 8¼"**
> (each stocking, not including hanging loop)

Materials

Materials are sufficient to make all 3 stockings.

4½" × 6½" piece of red wool for letters and ornament trim

3" × 4½" piece of green wool for ornament

1" × 1½" piece of gray wool for ornament hanger

2½" × 3" piece of cream wool for stripe on ornament

½ yard of red striped toweling for stocking fronts

⅜ yard of green cotton print for stocking backs and toes

¼ yard of 18"-wide lightweight fusible web

3 lengths, 8" each, of ½"-wide black ribbon for hanging loops

Embroidery floss or 12-weight pearl cotton in red, brown, green, olive, cream, and gray

12-weight wool floss in brown

3 red buttons, ⅜" diameter, for ornament*

Template plastic

The project shown features buttons available from Buttermilk Basin. See "Resources," page 79.

Making the Stocking Front and Back

1 Trace the stocking and toe patterns on page 14 onto template plastic. Cut out the templates.

2 On the right side of the toweling and centering the stripe along the length of the stocking template, trace around the template three times. Cut out the stockings on the drawn line. Make three stocking fronts.

3 Flip the template over and trace three reversed stockings on the right side of the green print. Trace around the toe template three times. Cut out the stockings and toes on the drawn line. Make three stocking backs and three toes.

Appliquéing the Design

1 Referring to "Wool Appliqué" on page 76, trace the patterns for the appliqués (page 15) onto the fusible web and prepare the wool shapes.

2 Referring to the photo on page 11 and using the stocking fronts, fuse the *J* on one stocking, the *Y* on another stocking, and the ornament on the remaining stocking.

3 Use one strand of pearl cotton to blanket-stitch the larger pieces in place, matching the floss color to the motif. On small pieces, you might prefer to use one or two strands of floss and a whipstitch. Wait to stitch the wire hanger on the ornament until after the branch is embroidered.

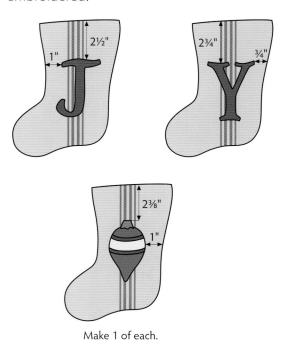

Make 1 of each.

Embellishing the Design

Refer to "Embroidery Stitches" on page 78 as needed and use three strands of floss throughout.

- **Stocking:** Place a green toe on each stocking and use red floss to blanket-stitch it in place as shown in the photo at left.

- **Branch:** Use brown wool thread to chain stitch the branch above the ornament. Use olive floss to stem-stitch the needles on the branch.

- **Wire hanger:** Stitch the wire hanger at the top of the ornament using gray floss and a chain stitch.

- **Buttons:** Sew the red buttons to the cream stripe on the ornament.

Finishing

1 Fold ½" of the stocking front top toward the wrong side and machine stitch across the top, about ¼" from the folded edge. Repeat for the stocking back. The raw edges will be on the inside of the stocking when the pieces are joined.

2 Use olive floss to sew a featherstitch (see the photo above right) about ¼" below the stitched line on the *J* and *Y* stockings.

3 With right sides together, join a stocking front and back, using a scant ¼" seam allowance. Clip the curves and corners and turn the stocking right side out. Make three stockings.

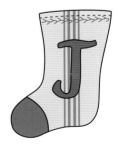

4 For each stocking, fold a piece of ribbon in half and sew it to the inside back seam to make the hanging loop.

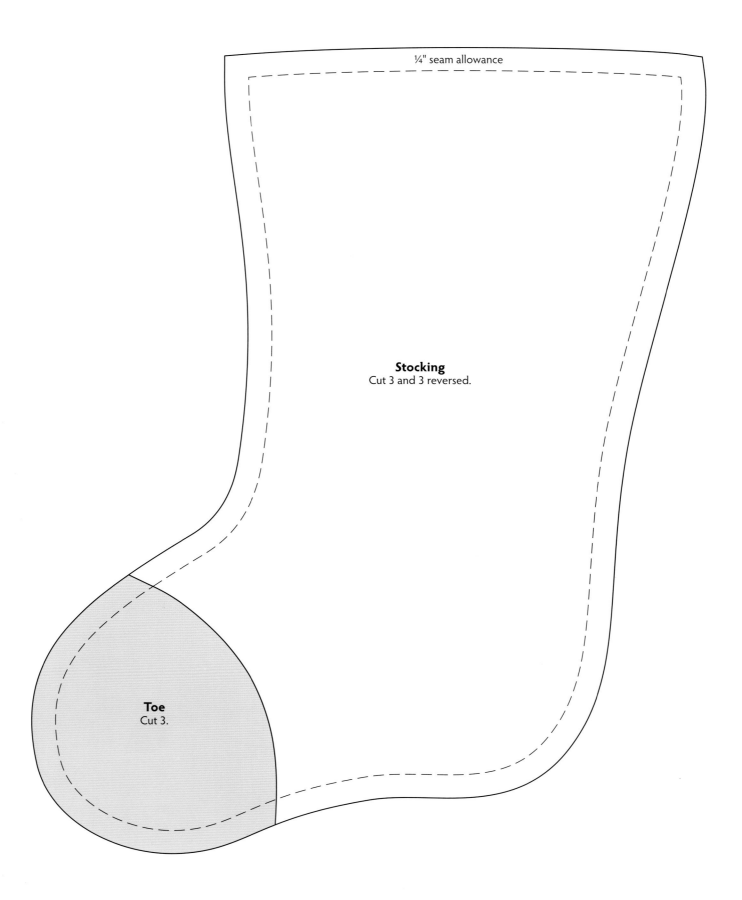

¼" seam allowance

Stocking
Cut 3 and 3 reversed.

Toe
Cut 3.

Patterns do not include seam allowances and are reversed for fusible appliqué.

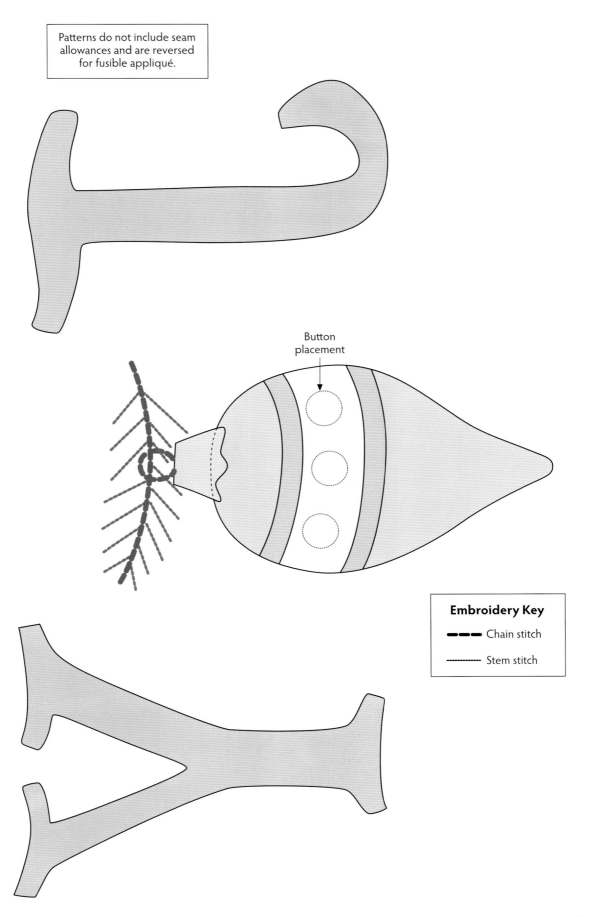

Button placement

Embroidery Key

━━━ Chain stitch

········· Stem stitch

Vintage VW Full of Cheer

Even if you've never struggled with hauling a Christmas tree home on a Beetle, I bet this image will make you smile. Those perfectly balanced packages tied up with string atop a white tree and retro red Bug—what's not to love?!

Finished size: 11" × 9"

Materials

2 rectangles, 9½" × 11½", of olive wool for pillow front and back

4" × 7½" rectangle of red plaid wool for car

4" × 5" rectangle of cream wool for tree and car windows

2" × 6" rectangle of red textured wool for hubcaps

1" × 4" rectangle of gray wool for running board

1½" × 3" rectangle of black wool for tires

1½" × 2¼" rectangle of gold wool for bottom present

1½" × 1½" square of rose wool for left present

1½" × 1½" square of red wool for top present

1½" × 2" rectangle of green wool for bow on bottom present

1" × 2" rectangle of brown wool for tree trunk

¼ yard of 18"-wide lightweight fusible web

Embroidery floss or 12-weight pearl cotton in red, brown, green, rose, gold, cream, black, and gray

4 tiny red buttons, 3 mm diameter, for bulbs on tree*

2 cream buttons, ⅜" diameter, for hubcaps*

1 gold button, ¼" diameter, for headlight*

12" length of black-and-cream twine

Fiberfill stuffing

The project shown features buttons available from Buttermilk Basin. See "Resources," page 79.

Appliquéing the Design

1 Referring to "Wool Appliqué" on page 76, trace the patterns for the appliqués (page 20) onto the fusible web and prepare the wool shapes.

2 Referring to the photo on page 18 and the pattern for placement, fuse the pieces to an olive green rectangle.

3 Blanket-stitch the larger pieces in place with one strand of pearl cotton, using gray around the tree and matching the floss color to the motif for the rest. On small pieces, you might prefer to use one or two strands of floss and a whipstitch.

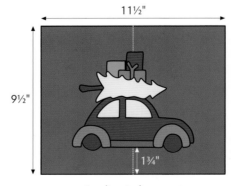

Appliqué placement

Finishing

1 With right sides together, align the pillow front with the remaining olive rectangle. Stitch the front and back together using a ¼" seam allowance, leaving a 3" opening to turn the pillow. Clip the corners and turn the pillow right side out.

Leave 3" open.

2 Stuff the pillow with fiberfill and stitch the opening closed.

GOT TWINE?

As each holiday arrives I love to shop the stores for various colors of twine. Not only does twine work great for embellishing your projects, it makes gift-wrapping a breeze. I wrap the presents in craft paper and simply tie them up in cute twine.

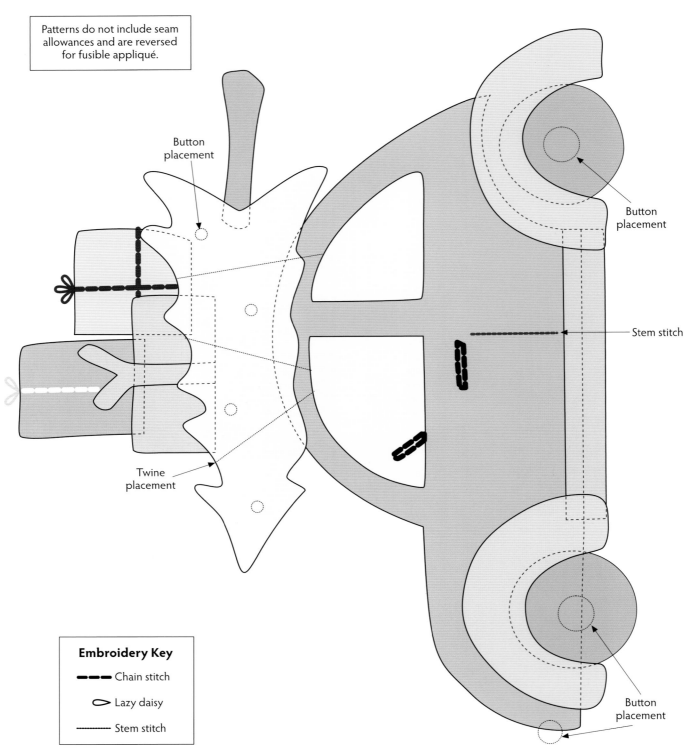

Patterns do not include seam allowances and are reversed for fusible appliqué.

Button placement

Button placement

Twine placement

Stem stitch

Button placement

Embroidery Key

▬▬▬ Chain stitch

⌒ Lazy daisy

·········· Stem stitch

Vintage VW Full of Cheer

Dec. 25 Sack

If you've never tried working with striped toweling, we encourage you to give it a try. You can find it in several colors and styles of stripes, and it makes a perfect backdrop for this little sack that shouts out the special day! Wouldn't it be fun to stitch these for your family members or sewing pals and hang the bags on their doors for a Christmastime surprise?

Finished size: 6" × 12"

Materials

3½" × 4½" rectangle of green wool for letters

4½" × 4½" square of black wool for numbers

2" × 2½" rectangle of textured green wool for leaves

1" × 18" strip of black print for cuff

2" × 18" strip of black print for cuff

1½" × 18" strip of red print for cuff

3½" × 18" strip of green print for cuff lining

⅓ yard of red striped toweling for sack body

⅛ yard of 18"-wide lightweight fusible web

1 yard of ½"-wide black ribbon for tie

Embroidery floss or 12-weight pearl cotton in green, black, and cream

1 red button, ⅜" diameter, for holly berry*

The project shown features a button available from Buttermilk Basin. See "Resources," page 79.

Appliquéing the Design

1 Referring to "Wool Appliqué" on page 76, trace the patterns for the appliqués (page 25) onto the fusible web and prepare the wool shapes.

2 Referring to the photo on page 22 and the appliqué placement guide on page 23, center the letters and numbers on a red stripe. Add the holly leaves. Fuse the appliqués in place.

3 Use one strand of pearl cotton to blanket-stitch the larger pieces in place, matching the floss color to the motif. On small pieces, you might prefer to use one or two strands of floss and a whipstitch.

Embellishing the Design

Refer to "Embroidery Stitches" on page 78 as needed and use three strands of floss throughout.

• **Cream floss:** Featherstitch veins on the leaves.

• **Button:** Sew the red button over the intersecting ends of the holly.

Assembling the Sack

Use a ¼" seam allowance for the following steps. Press all seam allowances in the direction indicated by the arrows.

1 Once the appliqué is completed, trim the toweling to measure 9½" tall, keeping the design centered from top to bottom. Measure 1½" to the right of the appliqué and trim off the hemmed edge. Measuring 12½" from the trimmed right edge, trim the left edge. The toweling should now measure 12½" × 9½".

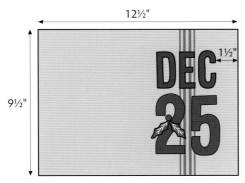

Appliqué placement

2 Fold the toweling in half, right sides together as shown. Stitch along the side and bottom edges of the sack. Zigzag or stitch ⅛" from the first stitched line to prevent raveling. Turn the sack right side out. The sack body should measure 6" × 9¼".

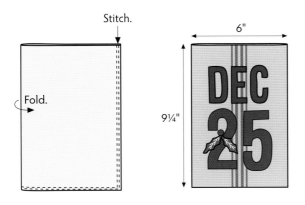

3 Sew the black strips to both long sides of the red strip. The outer cuff should measure 3½" × 18".

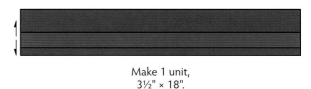

Make 1 unit, 3½" × 18".

4 Sew the green strip to the long side of the wider black strip. Fold the strip in half lengthwise to make a 3¼" × 18" cuff. Trim the cuff to measure 12½" long.

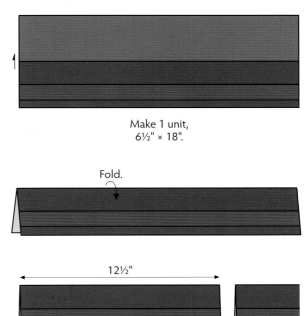

Make 1 unit, 6½" × 18".

5 Unfold the cuff. Refold, wrong sides together and with the short ends aligned. Join the short ends of the cuff, stitching on only the black and green strips, starting and stopping with a backstitch. Do not sew on the red strip as this will become the opening for the drawstring. Press the seam allowances open.

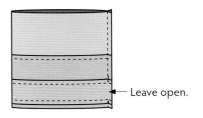

6 Slide the cuff over the sack body, aligning the raw edges. Pin in place. Sew around the top of the sack.

7 Fold under ¼" along the edge of the green lining and press to make a hem. Turn the lining inside the sack and pin to cover the cuff seam allowance. Hand stitch the folded edge in place.

8 On the right side of the sack, topstitch along both seamlines of the red strip to create a casing for the ribbon. Attach a large safety pin to one end of the ribbon and use it to thread the ribbon through the opening in the casing. Remove the pin and then tie a knot in both ends of the ribbon.

9 Align the ends of the ribbon to prevent it from being pulled out of the casing. On the opposite side of the casing opening, machine stitch across the red strip, starting and stopping with a backstitch to secure the ribbon.

Align raw edges.

DEC
25

Patterns do not include seam allowances and are reversed for fusible appliqué.

Button placement

Featherstitch

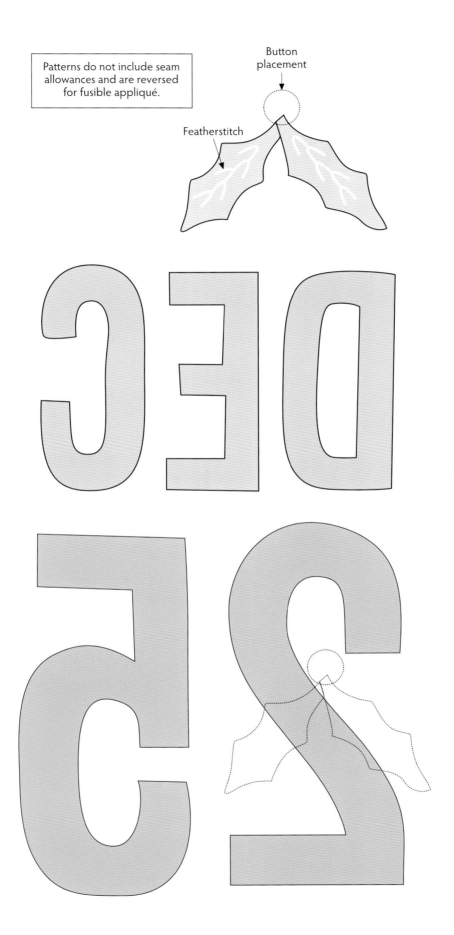

Vintage N*O*E*L

A sophisticated mistletoe wreath, ornate lettering, a vintage-style Christmas tree ornament, ribbon, and a candy cane are all welcome signs of the season. This piece, which is sure to become a family favorite, will give you plenty of opportunities to put your embroidery stitches to beautiful use.

Finished size: 18½" × 8½"

Materials

7" × 16½" rectangle of black wool for background

5" × 10½" rectangle of cream wool for letters

5" × 6" rectangle of green wool for wreath, holly leaves, and ornament trim

4" × 5" rectangle of red wool for candy cane, bow, and ornament

1" × 4½" rectangle of rose wool for candy cane stripes

2 rectangles, 9" × 19", of red print for runner top and back

¼ yard of 18"-wide lightweight fusible web

Embroidery floss or 12-weight pearl cotton in tan-and-cream twisted tweed, light green, dark green, red, rose, white, and gray

12-weight wool floss in dark green

6 cream buttons, ¼" diameter, for wreath*

1 cream button, ⅜" diameter, for bow*

3 tiny cream buttons, 3 mm diameter, for holly berries*

The project shown features buttons available from Buttermilk Basin. See "Resources," page 79.

Appliquéing the Design

1 Referring to "Wool Appliqué" on page 76, trace the patterns for the appliqués (pattern sheet 1) onto the fusible web and prepare the wool shapes.

2 Referring to the photo on page 29 and the pattern for placement, fuse the pieces to the black rectangle, keeping the design centered.

3 Blanket-stitch the word *NOEL* in place with one strand of pearl cotton, using gray around the letters and dark green for the wreath. On small pieces, you might prefer to use one or two strands of matching floss and a whipstitch.

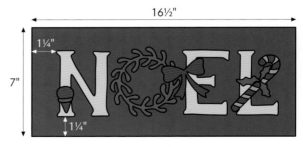

Appliqué placement

Embellishing the Design

Floss is 12-weight pearl cotton or six-strand embroidery floss unless otherwise specified. Refer to "Embroidery Stitches" on page 78 as needed and use three strands of floss throughout.

- **White floss:** Stitch the snowflake using a backstitch and straight stitches.

- **Dark green wool floss:** Use a chain stitch and straight stitches for the greenery.

- **Rose floss:** Make French knots on the ornament and backstitch lines on the red bow. Use lazy daisy stitches and stem stitches for the bow on the greenery, and featherstitch a line down the left side of the letter *N* and down the center of the letter *L*.

- **Gray floss:** Use chain stitches and a satin stitch to make the hanger on the ornament.

- **Buttons:** Sew the cream ¼" buttons to the wreath for berries, the small cream buttons to the holly leaves, and the cream ⅜" button to the bow.

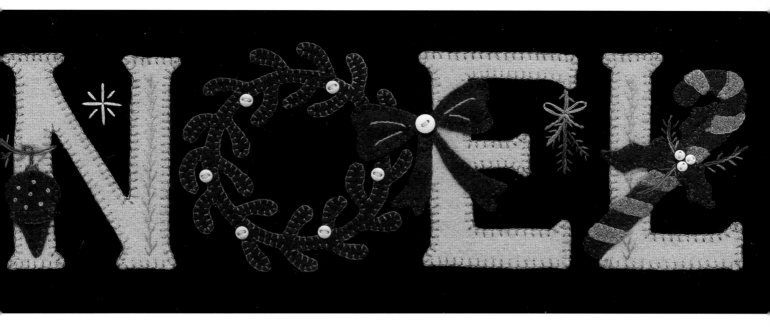

Finishing

1 Trim the appliquéd rectangle to measure 6½" × 16½", keeping the design centered. Center and pin the appliquéd rectangle on the right side of one red rectangle. Use three strands of gray floss to blanket-stitch around the perimeter to secure the appliquéd rectangle to the red background.

2 Pin the appliquéd piece and remaining red rectangle right sides together. Stitch the pieces together using a ¼" seam allowance, leaving a 4" opening to turn the runner.

3 Clip the corners and turn the runner right side out. Stitch the opening closed.

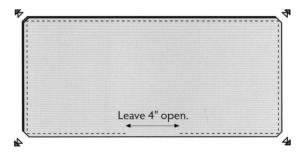

Trim.

Frosty Frolic Vintage Sack

Bedecked in a top hat and tweed scarf, Frosty is ready for fun.
Fill this sack with greens for door decor, or hang it from the mantel
to await Christmas goodies. Either way, it's sure to delight.

Finished size: 7½" × 15¾"

Materials

6" × 9" rectangle of green wool for tree

5" × 7½" rectangle of cream wool for snowman
and snow on hat

5½" × 8½" rectangle of cream houndstooth wool
for snow on ground

3½" × 4" rectangle of red textured wool for scarf

2" × 3½" rectangle of red wool for mittens
and hatband

2½" × 2½" square of black wool for hat

4" × 9" rectangle of red plaid wool for scallop trim

¼ yard of 16"-wide red stripe toweling for sack front

8" × 16¾" rectangle of cream plaid for sack back

⅜ yard of 18"-wide lightweight fusible web

Embroidery floss or 12-weight pearl cotton in green,
gray, red, black, rose, white, and tan-and-cream
twisted tweed

6 cream buttons, ⅜" diameter, for bulbs on tree*

6 red buttons, ⅜" diameter, for bulbs on tree*

2 black buttons, ⅜" diameter, for snowman's
tummy*

2 tiny black buttons, 3 mm diameter, for
snowman's eyes*

18" length of ½"-wide black ribbon for hanging

*The project shown features buttons available from
Buttermilk Basin. See "Resources," page 79.*

Appliquéing the Design

1 Referring to "Wool Appliqué" on page 76, trace
the patterns for the appliqués and scallop
trim (pattern sheet 2) onto the fusible web and
prepare the wool shapes.

2 Place the scallop on the toweling, aligning the
line on the pattern with the hemmed edge. Fuse
in place on the right side of the toweling. Fold
the top of the scallop over the hemmed edge;
fuse in place. Blanket-stitch along the scallops.

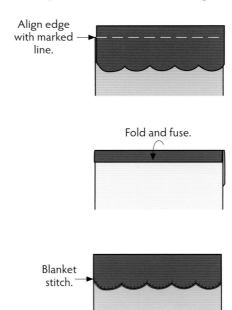

Align edge
with marked
line.

Fold and fuse.

Blanket
stitch.

3 Referring to the photo on page 31 and the pattern for placement, fuse the appliqués to the toweling.

4 Use one strand of pearl cotton to blanket-stitch the larger pieces in place, matching the floss color to the motif. On small pieces, you might prefer to use one or two strands of floss and a whipstitch.

Embellishing the Design

Refer to "Embroidery Stitches" on page 78 as needed and use three strands of floss throughout.

- **Tan-and-cream floss:** Featherstitch a line about ¾" from the top of the sack.
- **Black floss:** Chain stitch the *J* and *Y*. Make a French knot at the top of the *J*. Stem-stitch the snowman's mouth.
- **Green floss:** Chain stitch the wreath and the tree trunks on the snow. Straight stitch the tree branches.
- **Red floss:** Make French knots on the wreath. Satin stitch the nose. Stitch and tie fringe onto the ends of the scarf.
- **Rose floss:** Chain stitch the garland on the tree.
- **White floss:** Make French knots for snowflakes.
- **Gray floss:** Chain stitch the arm, feet, and tummy lines on the snowman.
- **Buttons:** Sew the red and cream buttons to the tree for bulbs. Sew the black 3 mm buttons to the snowman for eyes. Sew black ⅜" buttons to the snowman's tummy.

Assembling the Sack

1 Once the appliqué is completed, trim the sack front to measure 8" wide, keeping the design centered from side to side. Measuring from the top edge, trim the sack to measure 16" long.

Appliqué placement

2 Fold over ¾" on one 8" edge of the sack back and press. Topstitch along the raw edge to make a hem.

Make 1 back unit,
8" × 16".

3 Place the sack front and back right sides together. Stitch down one side, across the bottom, and up the other side, using a ¼" seam allowance. Zigzag or stitch ⅛" from the first stitched line to prevent raveling. Turn the sack right side out. The sack should measure 7½" × 15¾".

4 Inside the sack at each side seam, position a ribbon end about ¾" down. Hand stitch in place.

FRAY CHECK

Fray Check is an optional aid to use while you're doing wool appliqué. If you apply a very thin bead along the edge of your appliqué pieces prior to stitching, it will keep the edges from fraying and help your stitches lie nicely along the edge.

Frosty Frolic Picture

Just as fun as his wool counterpart on page 30, this embroidered Frosty will skate his way into your heart. And we promise, he won't melt!

> Finished size: 5" × 12"

Materials

8" × 15" rectangle of mottled cream print for background

Embroidery floss in black, rose, brown, gray, white, red, and olive

12-weight wool floss in green

2 tiny black buttons, 3 mm diameter, for snowman's eyes*

2 black buttons, ¼" diameter, for snowman's tummy*

Black Pigma pen or other fine-point permanent marker

Light box (optional)

5" × 12" black frame with 4½" × 11½" opening*

Clear packing tape, 2" wide

The project shown features a frame and buttons available from Buttermilk Basin. See "Resources," page 79.

Embroidering the Design

Floss is 12-weight pearl cotton or six-strand embroidery floss unless otherwise specified. Refer to "Embroidery Stitches" on page 78 as needed and use three strands of floss throughout.

1 Copy the pattern on page 37 and place it between the cream print and a light box or window. Trace the pattern onto the cream fabric using a permanent pen.

2 Embroider the design in the following order.

- **Gray floss:** Stem-stitch the snowman and his tummy line.

- **Black floss:** Stem-stitch the snowman's hat, mouth, and skates. Use a chain stitch for the *J* and *Y*. Make a French knot at the top of the *J*.

- **Olive floss:** Chain stitch the wreath circle. Stem-stitch the straight lines on the scarf.

- **Green wool floss:** Stem-stitch the Christmas tree, needles on the wreath, and tree branches.

- **Red floss:** Stem-stitch the hatband, mittens, scarf outline, scarf zigzags, and snowman's nose. Make French knots on the wreath. For ornaments, stem-stitch seven circles and then fill them in with a satin stitch. Stitch and tie fringe onto the ends of the scarf.

- **Rose floss:** Chain stitch the garland on the tree.

- **White floss:** For ornaments, stem-stitch six circles and then fill them in with a satin stitch. Stem-stitch the snow on the hat, chain stitch the snow on the ground, and make French knots for snowflakes.

- **Brown floss:** Chain stitch the Christmas tree's trunk.

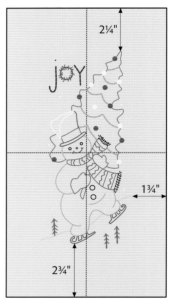

Embroidery placement

Finishing

1 Sew the tiny black buttons on the snowman for eyes. Sew the black ¼" buttons on the snowman's tummy.

2 Place the piece right side down on a flat surface. Place the cardboard insert from the frame on top, centering it over the embroidered piece. (You will need to create a 4¾" × 11¾" cardboard insert if your frame did not come with one.)

3 Fold the excess fabric over the cardboard and tape to secure it in place.

4 Insert the piece into the frame and replace the frame backing.

Stem stitch outline,
fill in with satin stitch.

Button
placement

Embroidery Key

- — — — Chain stitch
- • French knot
- ■ Satin stitch
- ········· Stem stitch
- —— Straight stitch

Yuletide Mini-Quilt

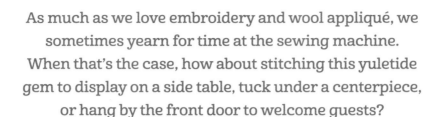

As much as we love embroidery and wool appliqué, we sometimes yearn for time at the sewing machine. When that's the case, how about stitching this yuletide gem to display on a side table, tuck under a centerpiece, or hang by the front door to welcome guests?

Finished size: 18¼" × 18¼"

Materials

Yardage is based on 42"-wide fabric. Fat eighths measure 9" × 21".

⅓ yard of green print for squares, setting triangles, and border

1 fat eighth of red floral for squares

1 fat eighth of cream check for squares

10" × 10" square of cream print for squares

10" × 10" square of gold print for squares

10" × 10" square of red print for squares

5" × 5" square of black print for squares

¼ yard of black solid for binding

⅔ yard of fabric for backing

23" × 23" piece of batting

Cutting

From the green print, cut:

1 strip, 1½" × 42"; crosscut into 20 squares, 1½" × 1½"

2 strips, 3" × 42"; crosscut into:

    2 strips, 3" × 18¼"

    2 strips, 3" × 13¼"

8 squares, 2¾" × 2¾"; cut into quarters diagonally to yield 32 side triangles

2 squares, 2⅜" × 2⅜"; cut in half diagonally to yield 4 corner triangles

From the red floral, cut:

3 strips, 1½" × 21"; crosscut into 36 squares, 1½" × 1½"

From the cream check, cut:

3 strips, 1½" × 21"; crosscut into 29 squares, 1½" × 1½"

From the cream print, cut:

24 squares, 1½" × 1½"

From the gold print, cut:

16 squares, 1½" × 1½"

From the red print, cut:

12 squares, 1½" × 1½"

From the black print, cut:

8 squares, 1½" × 1½"

From the black solid, cut:

2 strips, 2½" × 42"

2 Trim and square up the quilt top to measure 13¼" square, making sure to leave ¼" beyond the points of all the squares for seam allowances.

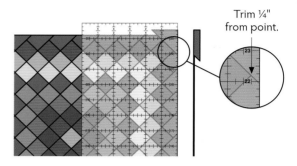

Trim ¼" from point.

Assembling the Quilt Top

Press all seam allowances in the direction indicated by the arrows.

1 Lay out the print 1½" squares in diagonal rows as shown. Add the green side and corner triangles. Sew the squares and side triangles together into rows. Join the rows to make the quilt-top center. Add the corner triangles last.

QUILT VERSATILITY

This is one of my favorite little quilts to make, and the colors can easily be switched out for a whole new look. Think tan, cream, and red for a more traditional or candy-cane look.

3 Sew the green 13¼" strips to opposite sides of the quilt top. Sew the green 18¼" strips to the top and bottom of the quilt top. The quilt top should measure 18¼" square.

Quilt assembly

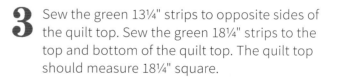

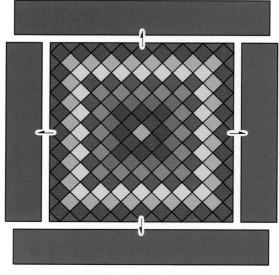

Adding borders

Finishing

For help with any of the following steps, go to ShopMartingale.com/HowtoQuilt for free, illustrated instructions. Refer to "Adding a Hanging Sleeve" on page 79 if you want to hang your quilt.

1 Layer the quilt top with the batting and backing. Baste the layers and quilt. The quilt shown is quilted with straight lines to form a square in each row of on-point squares. A feather motif is quilted in the border.

2 Trim the batting and backing even with the quilt top.

3 Using the black solid 2½"-wide strips, make and then attach the binding.

Bringing Home the Trees

You don't have to own a vintage truck to enjoy this piece. You can stitch yourself a red truck complete with wooden sides to haul home the trees—with no worry of driving it in the snow! For added fun, do as we did and display it on a sled—the ultimate vehicle for snow.

Finished size: 15¾" × 12"

Materials

8" × 14½" rectangle of black wool for background

3½" × 14½" rectangle of cream houndstooth wool for snow on ground

5½" × 6" rectangle of red wool for truck

3½" × 9" rectangle of green wool for middle tree, wreath, and step on truck

4" × 6" rectangle of olive for outer trees

2½" × 6" rectangle of brown textured wool for side bed of truck

1½" × 6" rectangle of dark brown wool for poles

2" × 5" rectangle of cream wool for snow on trees

2" × 3½" rectangle of black wool for tires

1" × 4" rectangle of gray wool for running board on truck

2½" × 3½" rectangle of red textured wool for front fender

2 rectangles, 12½" × 16¼", of green print for runner front and back

⅜ yard of 18"-wide lightweight fusible web

Embroidery floss or 12-weight pearl cotton in cream, green, red, black, brown, olive, tan-and-cream twisted tweed, and black-and-tan twisted tweed

5 tiny red buttons, 3 mm diameter, for berries on wreath*

2 cream buttons, ⅜" diameter, for hubcaps*

10" length of red-and-white twine

The project shown features buttons available from Buttermilk Basin. See "Resources," page 79.

Appliquéing the Design

1 Referring to "Wool Appliqué" on page 76, trace the patterns for the appliqués (pattern sheet 2) onto the fusible web and prepare the wool shapes.

2 Place the cream houndstooth rectangle on top of the black rectangle, overlapping them about ¼" along one long edge. Use cream floss to blanket-stitch along the overlapped edges.

---

3 Referring to the pattern for placement, fuse the pieces to the background from step 2.

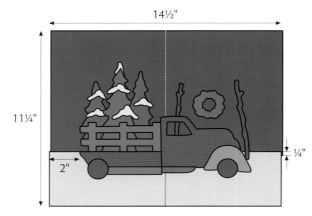

Appliqué placement

4 Use one strand of pearl cotton to blanket-stitch the larger pieces in place, matching the floss color to the motif. On small pieces, you might prefer to use one or two strands of floss and a whipstitch.

Embellishing the Design

Refer to "Embroidery Stitches" on page 78 as needed and use three strands of floss throughout.

- **Green floss:** Chain stitch the centerline of the greenery hanging on the poles; straight stitch the needles on the greenery. For the trees on the snow, chain stitch the tree trunks and use lazy daisy stitches for the branches.

- **Red floss:** Make French knots for berries on the greenery.
- **Black floss:** Chain stitch the handle on the door.
- **Tan-and-cream twisted tweed floss:** Stem-stitch the door line.
- **Cream floss:** Make French knots for snowflakes in the sky.
- **Red-and-white twine:** To make the hanger for the wreath, tack in place with cream floss.
- **Buttons:** Sew a cream button to the center of each tire. Sew the red buttons to the wreath for berries.

Finishing

1 Trim the appliquéd rectangle to 10" × 13¾", keeping the design centered. Center and pin the appliquéd piece to the right side of one of the green print rectangles. Use three strands of black-and-tan twisted tweed floss to blanket-stitch around the perimeter of the appliquéd black rectangle. Use tan-and-cream twisted tweed floss to blanket-stitch around the snow on the ground to secure the appliquéd rectangle to the green background.

2 Pin the appliquéd piece and remaining green print rectangle right sides together. Stitch the pieces together using a ¼" seam allowance, leaving a 4" opening to turn the runner. Clip the corners and turn the runner right side out. Stitch the opening closed.

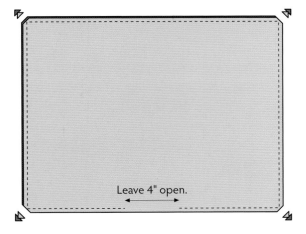

Leave 4" open.

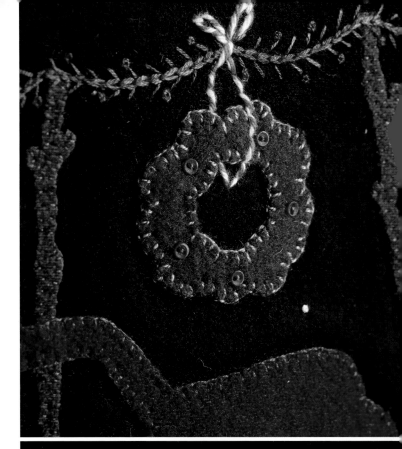

Candy Cane Stocking

Not much is sweeter at Christmas than a candy cane. This mini stocking is the perfect size to hang from a wreath—or to hold a special gift for your sweetheart.

> **Finished size: 6½" × 8"**
> (not including hanging loop)

Materials

3½" × 3½" square of rose wool for poinsettia

6" × 7" piece of red wool for poinsettia and candy cane

2" × 5" rectangle of cream wool for stripes on candy cane

1" × 1" square of gold wool for poinsettia center

10" × 16" rectangle of red striped toweling for stocking

⅛ yard of 18"-wide lightweight fusible web

Embroidery floss or 12-weight pearl cotton in red, cream, rose, and gold

12-weight wool floss in green

5 tiny black buttons, 3 mm diameter, for poinsettia center*

8" length of ½"-wide black ribbon for hanging loop

Template plastic

The project shown features buttons available from Buttermilk Basin. See "Resources," page 79.

Making the Stocking Front and Back

1 Trace the stocking on pattern sheet 2 onto template plastic. Cut out the template.

2 Place the template on the right side of the toweling, centering the stripe along the length of the stocking shape. Trace around the template. Cut out the stocking on the drawn line to make the stocking front.

3 Flip the template over and repeat step 2 to make the stocking back.

Appliquéing the Design

1 Referring to "Wool Appliqué" on page 76, trace the patterns for the appliqués (page 49) onto the fusible web and prepare the wool shapes.

2 Referring to the photo on page 47 and the pattern for placement, fuse the pieces to the stocking front.

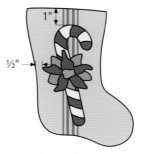

Appliqué placement

3 Use one strand of pearl cotton to blanket-stitch the larger pieces in place, matching the floss color to the motif. On small pieces, you might prefer to use one or two strands of floss and a whipstitch.

Embellishing the Design

Refer to "Embroidery Stitches" on page 78 as needed.

- **Green wool floss:** Stem-stitch the greenery sprigs.
- **Buttons:** Sew the black buttons to the center of the poinsettia.

Finishing

1 Fold the top of the stocking front ½" toward the wrong side and stitch across the top, about ¼" from the folded edge. Repeat for the stocking back. The raw edges will be on the inside of the stocking when the pieces are joined.

2 With right sides together, join the stocking front and back, using a scant ¼" seam allowance. Clip the corners and curves and turn the stocking right side out.

Clip.

3 Fold the piece of ribbon in half and sew it to the inside back seam for the hanging loop.

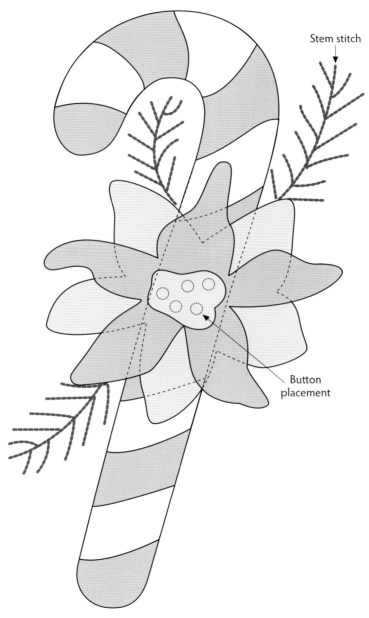

Patterns do not include seam
allowances and are reversed
for fusible appliqué.

Stem stitch

Button
placement

Candy Cane Stocking

Penny Rug Ornaments

Who says ornaments are just for trees? Deck the halls wherever you like with this trio of Santa, Frosty, and Miss Reindeer. Hand-stitched ornaments make perfect gift tags too.

Finished size: 4½" diameter

Materials

Materials are sufficient to make all 3 ornaments.

4½" × 13" rectangle of black wool for backgrounds

5" × 11" rectangle of rose wool for reindeer ornament base

5" × 12" rectangle of green wool for Santa ornament base, snowman's scarf, and collar on reindeer

6" × 12" rectangle of red wool for snowman ornament base, Santa's hat, snowman's hatband, and bow on reindeer

3½" × 5" rectangle of cream wool for snowman, Santa's mustache and hat trim

3½" × 3½" square of tan textured wool for Santa's coat and snowman's hat

1" × 1" square of orange wool for snowman's nose

2½" × 2½" square of gray houndstooth wool for Santa's beard

3" × 4" rectangle of brown wool for reindeer

2½" × 2½" square of light tan wool for reindeer's face

½ yard of 18"-wide lightweight fusible web

Embroidery floss or 12-weight pearl cotton in red, brown, rose, green, cream, black, orange, and tan

3 black buttons, ³⁄₁₆" diameter, for reindeer's nose and snowman's tummy*

5 tiny black buttons, 3 mm diameter, for reindeer's, snowman's, and Santa's eyes*

1 cream button, ³⁄₁₆" diameter, for reindeer's bow*

1 tiny red button, 3 mm diameter, for Santa's nose*

1 cream button, ¼" diameter, for pom-pom on Santa's hat*

30" length of black-and-cream twine for hangers

The project shown features buttons available from Buttermilk Basin. See "Resources," page 79.

Appliquéing the Designs

1 Referring to "Wool Appliqué" on page 76, trace the patterns for the appliqués and the background circles (pages 54 and 55) onto the fusible web and prepare the wool shapes.

2 Referring to the patterns for placement, fuse the appropriate pieces to each of the black background circles.

Appliqué placement

3 Use one strand of pearl cotton to blanket-stitch the larger pieces in place, matching the floss color to the motif. On small pieces, you might prefer to use one or two strands of floss and a whipstitch.

Embellishing the Reindeer Ornament

Refer to "Embroidery Stitches" on page 78 as needed and use three strands of floss throughout.

- **Cream floss:** Make French knots for snowflakes and straight stitch lines on the bow.
- **Red floss:** Make French knots on the collar.
- **Buttons:** Sew a 3 mm black button to the reindeer for an eye and a ³⁄₁₆" black button for a nose.

Embellishing the Snowman Ornament

- **Green floss:** Stem-stitch the greenery to the hat.
- **Cream floss:** Make French knot berries on the greenery and five on the background for snowflakes.
- **Black floss:** Make French knots for the snowman's mouth.
- **Red floss:** Stitch and tie fringe on the scarf.
- **Buttons:** Sew two 3 mm black buttons to the snowman for eyes and two ³⁄₁₆" black buttons to the front of the snowman.

Embellishing the Santa Ornament

- **Green floss:** Fly stitch a line across the middle of the hat trim.
- **Red floss:** Make French knots on the greenery.
- **Tan floss:** Stem-stitch lines on the beard.
- **Cream floss:** Make French knots on the background for snowflakes.
- **Buttons:** Sew the ¼" cream button to the end of the hat for a pom-pom. Sew two 3 mm black buttons to Santa for eyes and a 3 mm red button for his nose.

Finishing

1 Trace the base circle pattern (page 55) onto fusible web six times. Cut out the circles, leaving about ¼" outside the drawn lines.

2 Fuse two circles to the wrong side of each of the rose, green, and red rectangles. Cut out the circles on the drawn lines and peel away the paper backing.

3 Place the appliquéd reindeer in the center of one rose circle. Use one strand of tan pearl cotton to blanket-stitch around the black circle.

4 Fuse the second rose circle to the wrong side of the reindeer ornament. Use one strand of rose pearl cotton to blanket-stitch around the perimeter of the circles, through both layers.

5 Repeat step 3 to stitch the appliquéd Santa to the green circle and the appliquéd snowman to the red circle.

6 Fuse the second green circle to the wrong side of the Santa ornament. Use one strand of green pearl cotton to blanket-stitch around the perimeter of the circles, through both layers.

7 Fuse the second red circle to the wrong side of the snowman ornament. Use one strand of red pearl cotton to blanket-stitch around the perimeter of the circles, through both layers.

8 Cut the twine into three 10"-long pieces. Thread a needle with the twine and insert the needle in the top of an ornament. Tie a knot in the ends of the twine to make a hanger. Repeat for each ornament.

Penny Rug Ornaments

Patterns do not include seam allowances and are reversed for fusible appliqué.

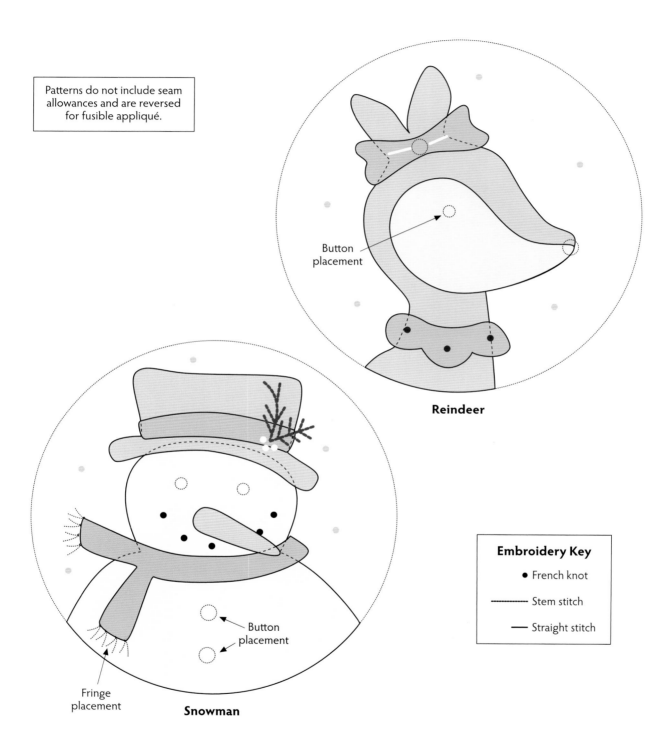

Button placement

Reindeer

Button placement

Fringe placement

Snowman

Embroidery Key

● French knot

- - - - Stem stitch

——— Straight stitch

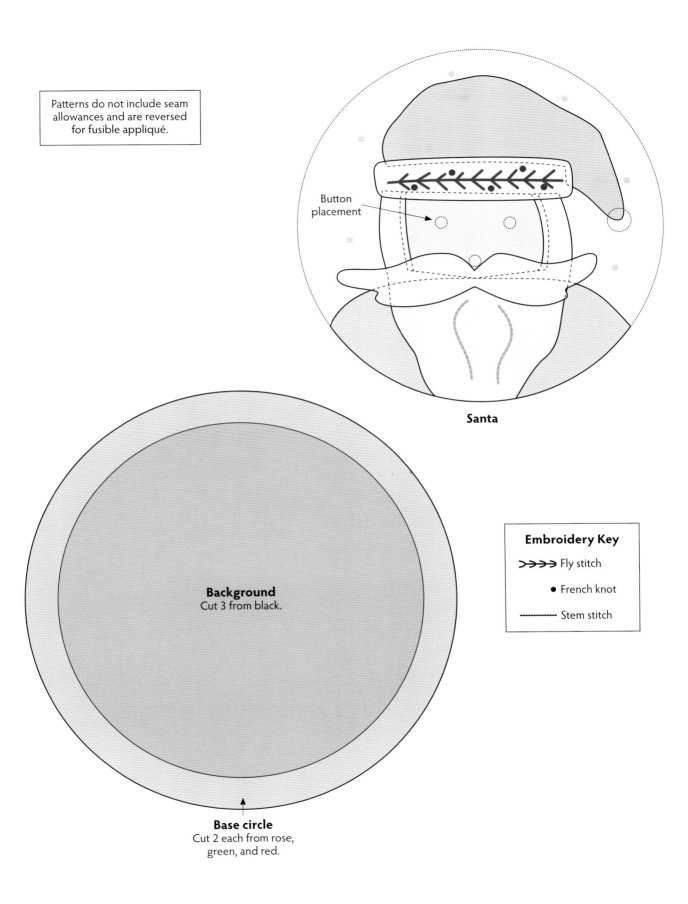

Patterns do not include seam allowances and are reversed for fusible appliqué.

Button placement

Santa

Background
Cut 3 from black.

Base circle
Cut 2 each from rose, green, and red.

Embroidery Key

>>>> Fly stitch

● French knot

----- Stem stitch

Holiday Mitten Quilt

When it's time to make the house merry with Christmas decor, start with a mitten you'll never lose! Spotlighted on a wall, centered on a table, nestled in a basket—where will your Holiday Mitten Quilt go?

> Finished size: 12½" × 12½"
> Finished block: 6" × 6"

Materials

Yardage is based on 42"-wide fabric. Fat quarters measure 18" × 21". Fat eighths measure 9" × 21".

3" × 4" rectangle of rose wool for mitten and candy cane stripes

3½" × 3½" square of cream wool for mitten cuff, candy cane, and candy stick

3" × 3" square of red wool for candy cane stripes, ornament, and mitten

3½" × 4" rectangle of dark green wool for holly leaves

2" × 3" rectangle of light green wool for tree

1" × 1" square of gold wool for hanger on ornament

1" × 1" square of brown wool for tree trunk

1 fat quarter of red print for block and binding

1 fat eighth of gold print for block

1 fat quarter of tan homespun for border

1 fat quarter of fabric for backing

17" × 17" square of cotton batting

⅛ yard of 18"-wide lightweight fusible web

Embroidery floss or 12-weight pearl cotton in green, red, rose, cream, gray, and tan-and-cream twisted tweed

12-weight wool floss in olive

3 red buttons, ¼" diameter, for holly berries*

12" length of black-and-cream twine

The project shown features buttons available from Buttermilk Basin. See "Resources," page 79.

Cutting

From the red print, cut:
2 squares, 2⅞" × 2⅞"
1 rectangle, 1½" × 10½"
3 strips, 2½" × 21"

From the gold print, cut:
2 squares, 2⅞" × 2⅞"
1 square, 2½" × 2½"
1 rectangle, 1½" × 10½"

From the tan homespun, cut:
2 strips, 3½" × 6½"
2 strips, 3½" × 12½"

Assembling the Quilt Top

Press all seam allowances in the direction indicated by the arrows.

1 Layer a red and a gold 2⅞" square right sides together and draw a diagonal line from corner to corner on the wrong side of the top square. Stitch a scant ¼" from each side of the marked line. Cut the unit apart on the marked line to make two half-square-triangle units. The units should measure 2½" square, including seam allowances. Make four units.

Make 4 units, 2½"× 2½".

2 Sew the red and gold rectangles together along one long edge to make a strip set that measures 2½" × 10½", including seam allowances. Crosscut the strip set into four 2½" square segments.

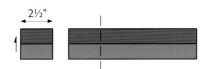

2½"

Make 1 strip set, 2½" × 10½".
Cut 4 segments, 2½" × 2½".

3 Lay out the half-square-triangle units, the segments from step 2, and the gold 2½" square in three rows, as shown. Sew the pieces into rows. Join the rows to make a 6½" square block, including seam allowances.

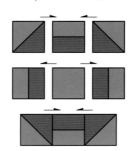 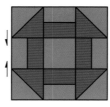

Make 1 block,
6½" × 6½".

4 Sew the tan 3½" × 6½" strips to the top and bottom of the block. Sew the tan 3½" × 12½" strips to opposite sides of the block. The quilt top should measure 12½" square.

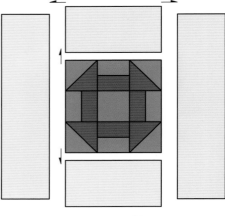

Quilt assembly

Appliquéing the Design

1 Referring to "Wool Appliqué" on page 76, trace the patterns for the appliqués (page 61) onto the fusible web and prepare the wool shapes.

2 Referring to the photo on page 59 and the pattern for placement, fuse the pieces to the quilt top.

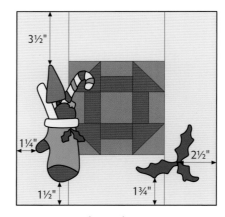

3½"

1¼"

2½"

1½"

1¾"

Appliqué placement

3 Use one strand of pearl cotton to blanket-stitch the larger pieces in place, matching the floss color to the motif. On small pieces, you might prefer to use one or two strands of floss and a whipstitch.

Embellishing the Design

Floss is 12-weight pearl cotton or six-strand embroidery floss unless otherwise specified. Refer to "Embroidery Stitches" on page 78 as needed and use three strands of floss throughout.

- **Olive wool floss:** Chain stitch the greenery stems coming out of the mitten and make lazy daisy stitches for the needles.

- **Rose floss:** Make French knots on the greenery coming out of the mitten.

- **Red floss:** Make French knots where the small holly leaves meet and stem-stitch lines on the candy-cane stick.

- **Cream floss:** Fly stitch a line down the middle of the tree.

- **Gray floss:** Chain stitch the hook on the ornament and straight stitch the lines on the ornament hanger.

- **Tan-and-cream twisted tweed floss:** Featherstitch a line across the mitten cuff, chain stitch a line on each small holly leaf, featherstitch

veins on the large holly leaves, and straight stitch lines at the bottom of the mitten.

- **Green floss:** Stem-stitch lines on the candy-cane stick.

MINI-QUILT ACCENT

If you'd like to add a mini-quilt accent to the center of the Churn Dash block, cut red and green 3½" squares from scraps and a 3½" square for backing. With right sides together, sew the red and green squares together around the outside edges using a ¼" seam. Cut the unit into quarters diagonally to make four triangle units. Trim the units to measure 2" square. Join the units to make a 3½" square Pinwheel block.

Place the block right sides together with the 3½" square of backing fabric. Stitch around the entire block, leaving a 1" opening for turning. Turn the block right side out and whipstitch the opening shut.

Using coordinating floss, attach the block to the center of the quilt top using a blanket stitch or featherstitch.

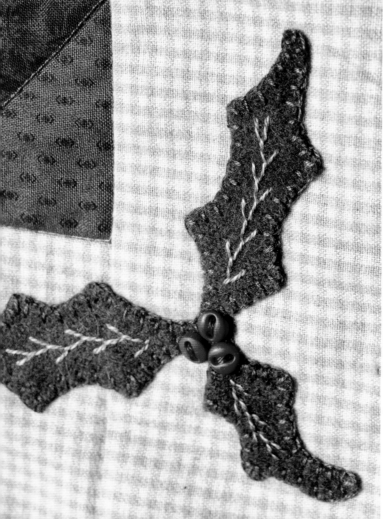

Finishing

For help with any of the following steps, go to ShopMartingale.com/HowtoQuilt for free, illustrated instructions. Refer to "Adding a Hanging Sleeve" on page 79 if you want to hang your quilt.

1 Layer the quilt top with the batting and backing. Baste the layers and quilt. The quilt shown is quilted in the ditch along the seamlines.

2 Trim the batting and backing even with the quilt top.

3 Using the red 2½"-wide strips, make and then attach the binding.

Patterns do not include seam
allowances and are reversed
for fusible appliqué.

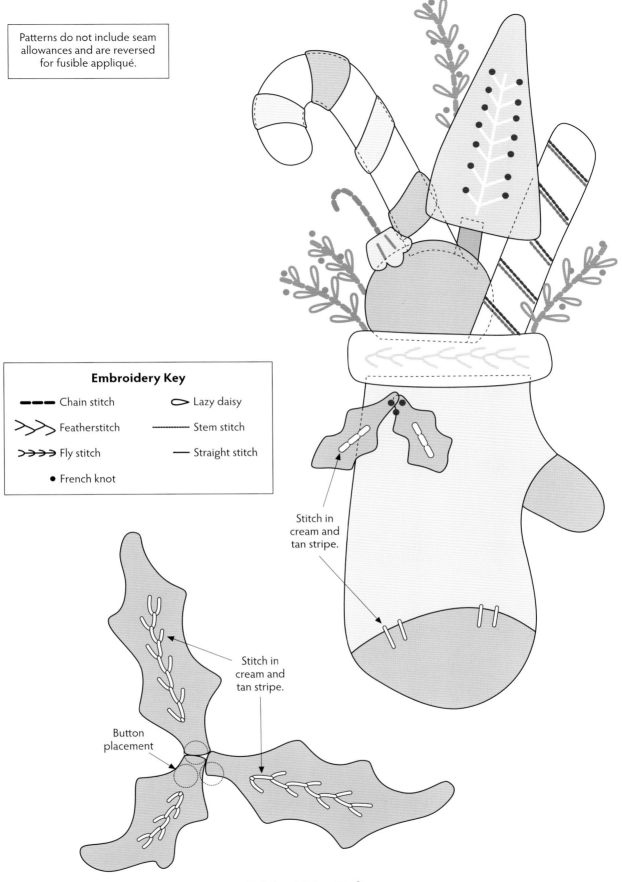

Embroidery Key

▬ ▬ ▬ Chain stitch   ◠ Lazy daisy

》》》 Featherstitch   ┄┄┄ Stem stitch

》》》》 Fly stitch   ── Straight stitch

● French knot

Stitch in
cream and
tan stripe.

Stitch in
cream and
tan stripe.

Button
placement

Holiday Mitten Quilt

Santa

Save your wool scraps because that's all you'll need to appliqué this little guy. If embroidery is more your thing, he looks equally dapper stitched in floss. Or, for a Santa-filled holiday, make them both! Really, can Christmas with two Santas be bad?

Santa in Wool

Framed finished size: 12" × 5"

Materials

8" × 15" rectangle of tan silk Matka for background*

2" × 4½" rectangle of textured green wool for letter *S*

2½" × 3" rectangle of eggshell wool for Santa's beard

3" × 3" square of textured cream wool for Santa's mustache and hat trim

3½" × 4" rectangle of red wool for letter *a* and Santa's hat

1½" × 1½" square of tan wool for Santa's face

2½" × 3" rectangle of plaid wool for letter *n*

3" × 4" rectangle of mottled green wool for feather tree

1" × 1" square of gold wool for star

⅛ yard of 18"-wide lightweight fusible web

Embroidery floss or 12-weight pearl cotton in green, red, cream, black, and gold

2 tiny black buttons, 3 mm diameter, for Santa's eyes*

1 cream button, ¼" diameter, for Santa's hat*

5" × 12" black frame with 4½" × 11½" opening*

Clear packing tape, 2" wide

Project shown features a frame, fabric, and buttons from Buttermilk Basin. See "Resources," page 79.

Appliquéing the Design

1 Referring to "Wool Appliqué" on page 76, trace the patterns for the appliqués (pattern sheet 1) onto the fusible web and prepare the wool shapes.

2 Referring to the photo on page 64 and the pattern for placement, fuse the pieces to the tan rectangle.

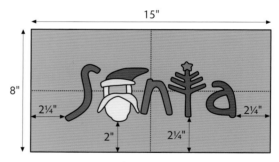

Appliqué placement

3 Use one strand of pearl cotton to blanket-stitch the larger pieces in place, matching the floss color to the motif. On small pieces, you might prefer to use one or two strands of floss and a whipstitch.

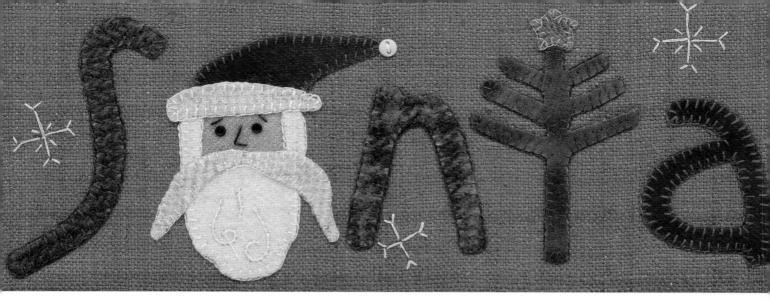

Embellishing the Design

Refer to "Embroidery Stitches" on page 78 as needed and use three strands of floss throughout.

- **Cream floss:** Straight stitch the snowflakes. Use a stem stitch for the lines on Santa's beard.

- **Black floss:** Straight stitch Santa's eyebrows and stem-stitch his nose.

- **Buttons:** Sew the cream button to Santa's hat for a pom-pom. Sew the black buttons to Santa's face for eyes.

Finishing

1 Place the piece right side down on a flat surface. Place the cardboard insert from the frame on top, centering it over the embroidered piece. (You will need to create a 4¾" × 11¾" cardboard insert if your frame did not come with one.)

2 Fold the excess fabric over the cardboard and tape to secure it in place.

3 Insert the piece into the frame and replace the frame backing.

Santa in Thread

Framed finished size: 12" × 5"

Materials

8" × 15" rectangle of mottled cream print for background

Embroidery floss in red, green, and brown

2 tiny black buttons, 3 mm diameter, for Santa's eyes*

Black Pigma pen or other fine-point permanent marker

Light box (optional)

5" × 12" black frame with 4½" × 11½" opening*

Tape

The project shown features a frame and buttons available from Buttermilk Basin. See "Resources," page 79.

Embroidering the Design

Refer to "Embroidery Stitches" on page 78 as needed and use three strands of floss throughout.

1 Copy the pattern on page 66 and place it between the cream print rectangle and a light box or window. Trace the pattern onto the cream fabric using the permanent pen.

2 Use red floss to chain stitch the letter *a*. Cross-stitch inside the *S*, the letter *n*, inside the hat trim and pom-pom, and inside the star.

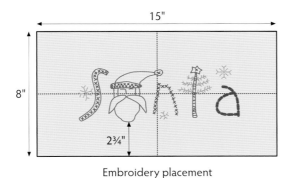

15"

8"

2¾"

Embroidery placement

3 Use brown floss to stem-stitch the tree.

4 Use green floss to stem-stitch the tree branches and snowflakes. Use straight stitches for the needles on the branches.

5 Sew black buttons to Santa's face for eyes.

Finishing

1 Place the piece right side down on a flat surface. Place the cardboard insert from the frame on top, centering it over the embroidered piece. (You will need to create a 4¾" × 11¾" cardboard insert if your frame did not come with one.)

2 Fold the excess fabric over the cardboard and tape to secure it in place.

3 Insert the piece into the frame and replace the frame backing.

FEWER TANGLES

Using shorter lengths of floss will make for fewer knots. Threading the needle more often is easier than having to frequently stop and untangle knots.

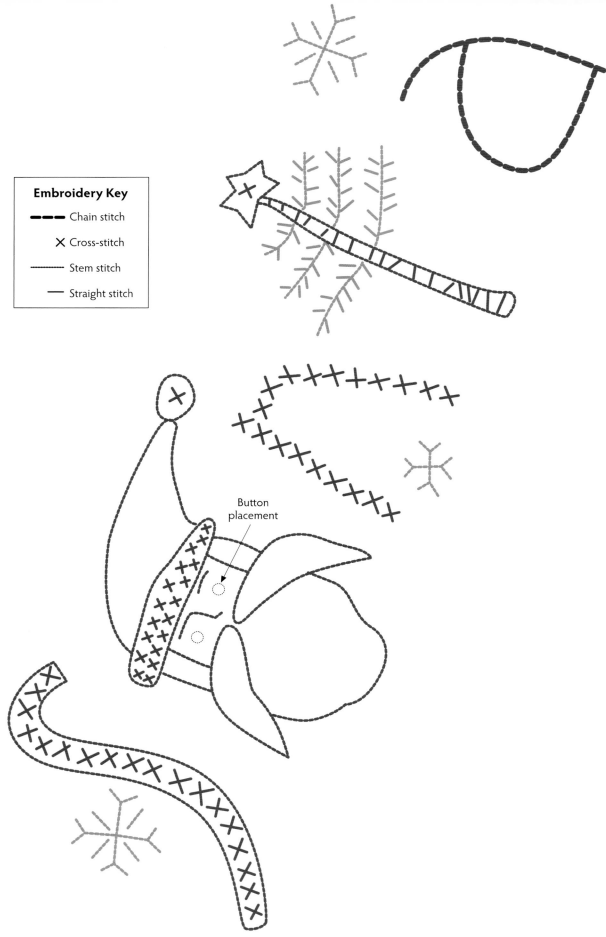

Embroidery Key

▬ ▬ ▬ Chain stitch

✕ Cross-stitch

· · · · · · · Stem stitch

— Straight stitch

Button
placement

Santa in Thread

Trio of Vintage Ornaments

Which is more fun? Stitching these sweet-as-can-be ornaments or displaying them on weathered metal stands? You may need to make more than three because your friends are sure to want one.

Framed size: 4" × 4" each

Materials

Materials are sufficient to make all 3 ornaments.

3 squares, 5" × 5", of black wool for background

3" × 5" rectangle of cream wool for snowmen and candy canes

1" × 2" rectangle of rose wool for trim on basket

2" × 3½" rectangle of red wool for snowmen's scarves and ornament

2½" × 2½" square of dark green wool for tree ornament and holly leaves

2" × 3½" rectangle of light green wool for tree

1" × 2" rectangle of brown wool for tree trunks

3" × 3½" rectangle of light brown plaid wool for basket

2" × 4½" rectangle of cream houndstooth wool for snow

1" × 1½" rectangle of gray wool for hat on snowman

⅛ yard of 18"-wide lightweight fusible web

Embroidery floss or 12-weight pearl cotton in red, gold, green, gray, black, cream, rose, orange, and brown

12-weight wool floss in olive

4 tiny black buttons, 3 mm diameter, for tummies

3 decorative frames with 3½" × 3½" opening*

The project shown features frames available from Buttermilk Basin. See "Resources," page 79.

Appliquéing the Design

1 Referring to "Wool Appliqué" on page 76, trace the patterns for the appliqués (page 71) onto the fusible web and prepare the wool shapes.

2 Referring to the photo on page 68 and the pattern for placement, fuse the appropriate pieces to each black square.

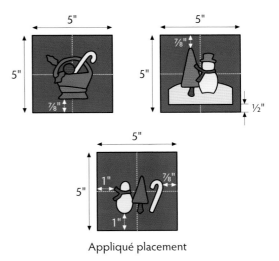

Appliqué placement

3 Use one strand of pearl cotton to blanket-stitch the larger pieces in place, matching the floss color to the motif. On small pieces, you might prefer to use one or two strands of floss and a whipstitch.

Embellishing the Basket Ornament

Floss is 12-weight pearl cotton or six-strand embroidery floss unless otherwise specified. Refer to "Embroidery Stitches" on page 78 as needed and use three strands of floss throughout.

- **Gold floss:** Stem-stitch a line for a vein on both holly leaves. Satin stitch the hanger on the ornament.
- **Olive wool floss:** Chain stitch the branches of the greenery and use lazy daisy stitches for the needles.
- **Red floss:** Make French knots for berries on the greenery and use chain stitches for the stripes on the candy cane.
- **Gray floss:** Chain stitch the hook on the hanger.

Embellishing the Hanging Ornaments

- **Red floss:** Stitch and tie fringe onto the ends of the scarf. Chain stitch stripes on the candy cane.
- **Black floss:** Make French knots for eyes on the snowman.
- **Orange floss:** Chain stitch the snowman's nose.
- **Cream floss:** Fly stitch a line down the middle of the tree.
- **Green floss:** Chain stitch the branches of the greenery and use lazy daisy stitches for the needles.
- **Rose floss:** Make French knots for berries on the greenery.
- **Gray floss:** Chain stitch hangers from the greenery to the ornaments.
- **Buttons:** Sew two 3 mm black buttons to the snowman's tummy.

Embellishing the Snowman with Tree Ornament

- **Cream floss:** Fly stitch a line down the middle of the tree and make French knots for snowflakes.
- **Brown floss:** Chain stitch and straight stitch twig arms on the snowman.
- **Red floss:** Chain stitch a band on the hat; stitch and tie fringe onto the ends of the scarf.
- **Black floss:** Make French knots for eyes on the snowman.
- **Orange floss:** Chain stitch the snowman's nose.
- **Gray floss:** Chain stitch the snowdrift at the bottom of the snowman.
- **Buttons:** Sew two 3 mm black buttons to the snowman's tummy.

Finishing

1 Trim each appliquéd square to measure 4½" square.

2 Place the piece right side down on a flat surface. Place the cardboard insert from the frame on top, centering it over the embroidered piece. (You will need to create a 4" × 4" cardboard insert if your frame did not come with one.)

3 Fold the excess fabric over the cardboard. Insert the cardboard into the frame and fold the metal clips over the cardboard to secure it in place.

TRIO OF IDEAS!

The vintage ornaments in this set have endless options. Here are my top three variations, to gift or to keep and enjoy!

- How cute would these be made into little pillows?

- Stitch them up, space 1" apart on a red print, and make into a runner.

- Simply add a coordinating wool background and make into ornaments to trim the tree.

Patterns do not include seam
allowances and are reversed
for fusible appliqué.

Satin stitch

Stitch in
gold.

Basket ornament

Fringe
placement

Hanging ornaments

Button
placement

Embroidery Key

▬▬▬ Chain stitch

➤➤➤➤ Fly stitch

● French knot

⬯ Lazy daisy

∙∙∙∙∙ Stem stitch

— Straight stitch

Fringe
placement

Button
placement

Snowman with Tree ornament

Wool Appliqué, Embroidery, and More

 As you have probably gathered by now, wool is my favorite medium to work in! There's something about wool that brings joy to my heart. I think my passion for it stems from growing up with generations of family members, including my great-grandparents. During the long winters here in Minnesota, there never was a day that Great-Grandma Lily wasn't donning her wool coat and fur hat, while many of the men in the family sported buffalo plaid wool hats and coats. Over the years, wool has remained constant in an ever-changing world, making it a traditional staple in the handwork community.

Although I would never cut into my great-grandmother's wool coat, many stitchers do glean wool from old coats. I prefer to work with my line of wool from Henry Glass and a few select hand-dyed wool pieces from various artists. When I was designing my line of wool for Henry Glass, I wanted

to create a palette that was reminiscent of the vintage colors that were often seen back in the day. I also wanted to make sure it was 100% wool, so it's perfect for artists who want to overdye and for those of us who prefer to felt it up. Working with 100% wool is always your best option, but I would never pass up a fabulous piece simply because it was a blend.

I also feel it's important to incorporate various textures or styles of wool into my work. Therefore, I made sure to include gorgeous plaids and herringbone patterns in my line. These really bring dimension to projects. They also add a nice contrast to the solid pieces of wool and allow you to make certain pieces pop; try switching to a textured piece of wool in the same color. Giving dimension to your work makes it more appealing to the eye, so never be afraid to mix and match!

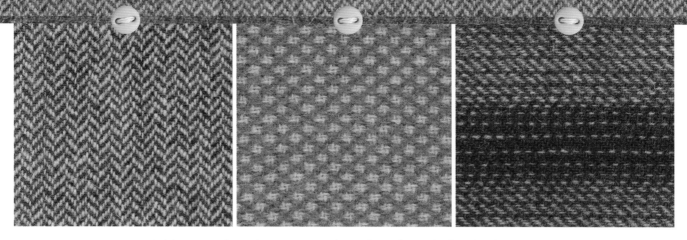

Add texture by using patterned wool, such as the herringbone, honeycomb, and striped twill weave pieces shown here.

Types of Wool

There are three types of wool used for wool appliqué. The first is vintage or repurposed wool; the second is new, off-the-bolt wool; and the third is hand-dyed wool. You can use any of these options for the projects in this book. At Buttermilk Basin, we use 100% wool in our projects. The only time I make an exception is when I stumble upon a fabulous vintage piece and just have to use it, even though it may not be 100% wool.

Vintage or repurposed wool. You may recall your grandmother wearing wool skirts years ago. Those skirts tend to be lighter-weight wool, but they offer unique textures and colors. They would be perfect to felt and use in your projects. You may also remember those gorgeous wool army blankets that got much use over the years. Those are heavier weight and would work best for backgrounds or to make into Christmas stockings. Many wool items for repurposing can be found at thrift stores or estate sales. If you choose to work with vintage wool, just be sure that it's clean, 100% wool. Felt it as necessary before using it in your projects.

New, off-the-bolt wool. This is any new wool available in your local quilt shop or online, such as my line with Henry Glass and Riley Blake Designs. It can usually be found in two widths, 45" or 52". The width varies by manufacturer. This type can be found in many colors, textures, and weights, from suit weight to coat weight. When purchasing our wool or any wool from a bolt, you will need to felt it before using it in your projects, just like vintage wool. See "Felting Wool" on page 74 for directions.

Hand-dyed wool. Hand-dyed wool is stunning! There is simply no other way to describe it. The artist starts out with a piece of vintage or bolt wool and mixes dyes, water, and vinegar to create a one-of-a-kind piece of wool. During the dye process the wool also gets felted, so you do not have to felt hand-dyed wool after your purchase. Since vinegar is used in this process, the wool also becomes colorfast, making it perfect to use in any project! These pieces of wool are often mottled and you can see many different colors within one piece, which makes it fun to work with. One of the downsides to hand-dyed wool is that each piece is unique, making it difficult to re-create if you need or want more. Another downside is that the process is time consuming, so the wool tends to be expensive. Regardless, I never pass up a unique piece of wool to add to my stash!

Felting Wool

First off, felting wool is easy. All you need to felt wool is a washing machine! Your washing machine provides the three things needed for felting: agitation, heat, and moisture. Felting is basically a process that entwines or locks the fibers together, turning the fabric into a felt-like piece.

To felt wool, use a small amount of laundry detergent and the normal wash cycle, with hot water followed by a cold rinse. After washing, put the wool in the dryer on hot until it is completely dry. It's always best to keep like colors together, as dark colors may bleed during the felting process. This also ensures that you won't have dark lint fibers adhering to light fabrics, so you keep the wool looking nice. Be sure to clean the lint trap of your dryer often, as fibers build up quickly.

When you felt wool, it's hard to know how much it will shrink in the process, and the results may vary from one wool to another. Shrinkage will generally range from 10% to 20%. Differences can be due to settings used during the felting process, such as how hot the water is and how long the wool is agitated, for example. The more you felt wool, the better you'll be able to predict shrinkage. For best results, use 100% wool whenever possible.

Supplies for Wool Appliqué

The best part about working with wool is that you need very few supplies and no fancy gadgets! In fact, once you learn the technique and prepare the appliqués, all you need to finish your project will be scissors, thread, and a needle. How cool is that?

FUSIBLE WEB

Since my technique uses fusible web, you won't need the freezer paper, templates, or glue sticks that some methods require. All you need is a package of Soft Fuse Premium fusible web. Soft Fuse is the *only* product I use when creating wool projects.

Soft Fuse is a paper-backed fusible web for both machine and hand appliqué. The main reason I *love* working with it is that it does not gum up the needle. You can stitch through it with ease, making for a pleasant stitching process. It also makes your project portable once the pieces are fused in place. Soft Fuse comes in various sizes, starting with 8" × 9" sheets in a package of 10 for smaller projects and in widths starting at 18" for larger projects.

NEEDLES

When it comes to needles, I suggest chenille needles. I use chenille needles in two sizes, 20 and 22. These needles are designed with a long, large eye and a sharp tip, making them easy to work with when using floss in heavier weights. The long eye is less abrasive on the thread, and the sharp tip creates a hole in the wool that allows the thread to pass through easily. An added bonus is that these needles make threading your needle a breeze! With that being said, I strongly encourage you to select whatever needles you feel most comfortable using.

MARKING TOOLS

The right tools make marking simple to do and easy to see on your fabrics.

Pencils. I always have a package of mechanical pencils on hand. I like sharp pencils to trace the pattern shapes onto the fusible web. Mechanical pencils also eliminate the need to have a sharpener on hand. I like a nice, crisp line so that I can easily see it when cutting out the shapes.

Marking pens. To mark on wool, a White Marking Pen (Fine) by Clover and a chalk pen are two of the items many of my students like using. These pens work great for drawing on dark fabrics or wool, and both pens are water soluble, making the marks easy to remove.

IRON

When choosing an iron, my only suggestion is to have an iron with steam. You'll need to use steam when fusing the appliqués.

THREADS AND FLOSS

These days, there's no end to the options for the type and weight of thread and floss to use. This is a good thing, but at times it may be overwhelming. To begin, I suggest using pearl cotton, six-strand embroidery floss, and wool thread. Within these three types, you'll have plenty of choices to enhance your projects. The more you stitch, the more you can learn and play with thread and floss. They can become another design element to enhance your projects.

Pearl cotton. I do 90% of my stitching with 12-weight pearl cotton, which is comparable to three strands of embroidery floss. I love this weight and find that I can use it on most any project. The best part is that it comes in both solids and hand-dyed colors. My preference, nine times out of ten, would be hand-dyed colors. I love how the shades flow on the wool.

Six-strand embroidery floss. I rarely complete a project without including a few of the standard, often-used colors of embroidery floss. I use two strands of floss for the smaller details, because using less floss helps to maintain the shape of little pieces. Like pearl cotton, there are both solid and hand-dyed options for embroidery floss.

Wool floss. Over the last couple of years, there has been a surge of wool floss on the market. Just like the two options of floss mentioned above, wool floss is available in different weights and colors. I'm just beginning to use more wool floss, and I'm pleased with the way it brings a new twist to my projects. Again, I would encourage you to use what you have and to experiment with new options that become available.

Wool Appliqué

Because the projects are made using the fusible-appliqué method, all of the appliqué patterns are reversed. Follow these steps for fusible appliqué.

1 Place the fusible web, paper side up, over the pattern.

2 Trace each pattern piece separately. If one shape overlaps another, be sure to include the extra wool that goes underneath, as shown by dashed lines in the patterns. When tracing the pattern pieces, leave approximately ¼" of space between the traced shapes, and label each one. If you have pattern pieces that will be cut from the same piece of wool, trace them close together on the fusible web.

Fusible web

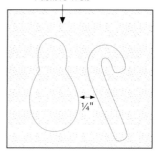

¼"

3 Roughly cut out each piece, leaving at least ⅛" around the traced lines. You can keep together as a unit all shapes that are to be cut from the same wool.

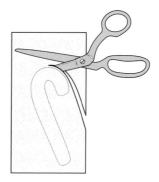

4 With the paper (traced) side up, lay the shapes close together on the chosen piece of wool but do not overlap them. Using your iron, fuse the paper pieces to the wool, following the manufacturer's instructions. While most wool is the same on both sides, take care to fuse the pieces to the side that you want to be the wrong side.

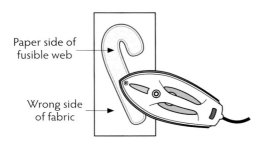

Paper side of fusible web

Wrong side of fabric

5 After the shapes have cooled, cut them out on the drawn line.

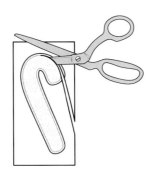

6 Referring to the pattern and the project photo, arrange the pieces on the background. When you have all of the pieces arranged, remove the paper backing from each wool piece and place the piece back in the layout. Be sure the pieces are layered correctly. Carefully press down on the pieces with a hot iron, using lots of steam to secure the appliqués in place. Press down for just a few seconds, and then gently move

the iron around to fuse all the pieces in place. It's important to use a lot of steam, as the fusible web needs to melt between the wool pieces to secure them in place. You can always go over them again if there's a piece or two that did not fuse securely. When everything is fused, turn over the entire piece and steam it from the back.

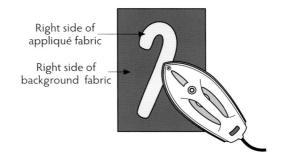

Right side of appliqué fabric

Right side of background fabric

7 After the piece cools, stitch around the appliqués using a blanket stitch or whipstitch.

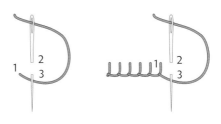

Blanket stitch

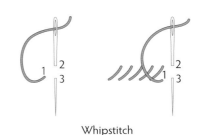

Whipstitch

Embroidery

When stitching the embroidered designs in this book or embellishing your wool projects, feel free to be creative and use the stitches you prefer in whatever colors and types of floss you prefer. That is the beauty of handwork! If you're unfamiliar with embroidery, refer to "Embroidery Stitches" below.

To transfer an embroidery design onto the background fabric, you need a light source such as a window or light box.

Lay the pattern on the light box or tape it to a window. Position the fabric over the pattern; trace the design lightly with a black or brown permanent fine-point marking pen. Use a fine-point marker so the lines won't show after you've stitched over them.

Embroidery Stitches

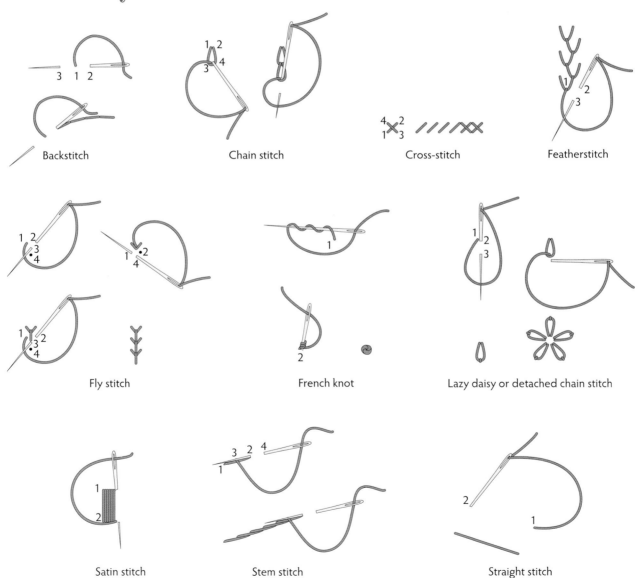

Backstitch

Chain stitch

Cross-stitch

Featherstitch

Fly stitch

French knot

Lazy daisy or detached chain stitch

Satin stitch

Stem stitch

Straight stitch

Adding a Hanging Sleeve

1 Before sewing the binding on, measure across the top edge of the quilt. Cut a 6"-wide fabric strip 1" longer than the measurement.

2 Fold under ¾" on the short ends, toward the wrong side of the fabric. Stitch ½" from the fold to create a hem.

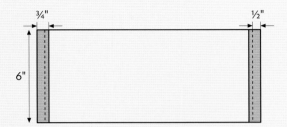

3 Fold under ¾" along one long edge of the strip and stitch ½" from the fold.

4 Place the strip on the back of the quilt, with the wrong side facing the quilt back and the raw edge along the top edge. Pin in place.

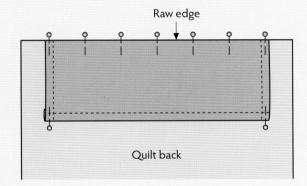

Raw edge

Quilt back

5 As you sew the binding on, you will sew the top of the sleeve to the quilt. Pin and stitch the bottom edge of the sleeve to the quilt by hand, being careful to stitch through the backing and batting only, not the front of the quilt.

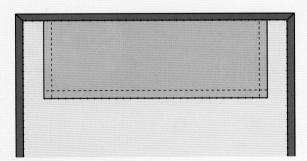

RESOURCES

Buttermilk Basin Design Studio

8535 Central Avenue NE #102
Spring Lake Park, MN 55434

ButtermilkBasin.com

Buttons, wool, yarn-dyed homespuns, cotton prints, patterns, and kits

About the Author

Stacy West is an artist who grew up in rural Minnesota surrounded by three generations of creative women. She learned to sew at an early age and studied graphic design in college. Stacy has never strayed far from fabrics and crafts as she worked at the local Ben Franklin in town, vended at numerous craft shows with her mother, and continued to work in a fabric store after college while designing for various craft magazines and continuing to sell her handcrafts.

In 1999, she and her mother, her partner in stitching and crafting, displayed and sold their wares from a booth at the International Quilt Market in Minneapolis, Minnesota. Stacy has been growing her business, Buttermilk Basin, featuring her original designs in wool and cottons. With products available online and at her thriving shop in Spring Lake Park, Minnesota, Buttermilk Basin is both a retail business selling wool, patterns, kits, fabrics, and home goods, as well as a wholesale supplier of her line of vintage-inspired patterns.

Stacy has become recognized as an innovator, a nationally known teacher, and a prolific designer in the quilting industry. She hosts three-day fiber retreats twice a year, and her work has appeared in a variety of magazines, including *Simply Vintage*, *American Patchwork & Quilting*, and *Quilts and More*. She and her husband, George, have two daughters, Hannah and Grace, who love being a big part of Stacy's creative journey!